THE RAPE OF 2,500 CREDITORS BY THE UNITED STATES JUDICIAL SYSTEM

THE RAPE OF 2,500 CREDITORS BY THE UNITED STATES JUDICIAL SYSTEM

✦

(an Exposé)

Corroborated and Documented by the CITIZENS FOUNDATION FOR A CANCER FREE AMERICA, INC.
www.cancerfreeamerica.net

iUniverse, Inc.
New York Lincoln Shanghai

THE RAPE OF 2,500 CREDITORS BY THE UNITED STATES JUDICIAL SYSTEM
(an Exposé)

iUniverse books may be ordered through booksellers or by contacting:

iUniverse
2021 Pine Lake Road, Suite 100
Lincoln, NE 68512
www.iuniverse.com
1-800-Authors (1-800-288-4677)

Volunteers of the Foundation reviewed litigation records, letters, notes, newspaper articles, press releases and many other documents. Based on the available material, the analyses and conclusion are believed to be substantially logical and accurate.

ISBN: 0-595-34745-2

Printed in the United States of America

Contents

Foreword

This exposé describes how the Citizens Foundation for a Cancer Free America, Inc. (Foundation) was denied $75 million. The Foundation believes that the United States Judicial System is well conceived, and most often directed by honest and dedicated judges and lawyers. When a human body malfunctions, it is often caused by cancer. The Judicial System, like the human body, has developed a cancer in a small area of its system, which this document will address. One small area of cancer can destroy the human body, or destroy an entire Judicial System if it is allowed to spread.

This cancer caused 2,484 individuals and companies to be denied $335,861,924. Two thousand of those individuals are senior citizens who planned to use the funds due them for retirement. Seventy-five million dollars of that amount was to be used for cancer research to develop the use of alternative medicine in conjunction with conventional methods to treat cancer. More than a third of cancer patients in Europe use alternative medicine. A substantial amount was earmarked for Johns Hopkins Hospital to supplement a National Institute of Health (NIH) grant to research the use of alternative medicine.

Described herein is how judges and lawyers in one infested area violated the Federal Rules of Civil Procedure, and warped the Judicial System, for no economic purpose, whatsoever.

The following is only a brief summary. Every fact has been reviewed. Lengthy bibliographies have been purposely omitted. Much detail lies behind each paragraph of the exposé. Many people that were involved, as well as people who should have been involved, are listed under "Acknowledgments."

This one occurrence, if not corrected, could be repeated on a daily basis throughout the country. Only with knowledge of what has happened in this one instance, can corrections be made.

What occurred is contrary to the United States Constitution and the laws established by Congress.

Chapters One through Five describe the thinking and attitudes that caused the Judicial System to malfunction.

Chapter Six describes what occurred and have been analyzed, corroborated and reviewed.

Acknowledgement To:

CONGRESSMAN BENJAMIN L. CARDIN
UNITED STATES CONGRESSMAN FROM MARYLAND

Congressman Cardin is the sole United States federal legislator who has demonstrated concern over what has occurred and has forwarded the material described in this publication to the:

HOUSE JUDICIARY COMMITTEE

The matter has adversely affected many associated people, and prevented additional research to cure cancer by the application of alternative and conventional medical procedures, used concurrently.

Fortuitous Acknowledgements:

The Foundation and Creditors note that the following Federal District Court Judges of the Fourth Circuit of the United States District Court for the District of Maryland appear to demonstrate partiality:

Judge William D. Quarles, Jr.
Judge Benson Everett Legg

These judges were formerly partners in the Baltimore law firm of Venable, Baetjer and Howard, LLP that represented a client who with co-participants, caused $335 million of damages to Creditors. The denial of all motions filed on behalf of the Creditors is not only remarkable, but gives the appearance of loyalty and preference to their prior relationship.

The Foundation and Creditors note that the following judges of the United States Court of Appeals for the Fourth Circuit appear to condone non-acceptable behavior:

Judge Clyde H. Hamilton
Judge Karen J. Williams
Judge William B. Traxler, Jr.
Judge William W. Wilkins

These Judges denied the Foundation's Motion to remove Judge James Schneider from his seat on the Bankruptcy Court, and denied an appeal of a Mandamus that would have required lower courts to answer four motions, one unanswered as of Christmas, 2004, for

460 days, one for 432 days, one for 320 days and the last for 265 days.

One law firm located in a large West Coast City, with five offices in other major cities throughout the country, that handles all litigation on a contingent basis, stated that they would not take a case that involved the United States District Court for the District of Maryland or that had to be appealed in the United States Court of Appeals for the Fourth Circuit in Richmond, Virginia due to knowledge of identical experiences that the Creditors and Foundation have been exposed to.

The actions of these seven judges made it possible, on October 7, 2004, to file a Writ of Certiorari before the Supreme Court of the United States where according to Article III of the United States Constitution, all judicial power is vested. The Certiorari requested, in addition to lower courts answering outstanding motions, that the Supreme Court protect 2,484 Creditors by correcting what transpired in the Fourth Circuit Federal Judicial system.

The Writ of Certiorari before the Supreme Court was denied on December 13, 2004, sixty-seven days after being filed, by a letter signed by William K. Suter, Clerk (not to be confused with Justice David Hackett Souter).

The Foundation and Creditors note that the following nine Justices of the U. S. Supreme Court appear to be both condoning and eliminating existing procedures:

Stephen Breyer
Ruth Bader Ginsburg
Anthony M. Kennedy
Sandra Day O'Connor
William Hubbs Rehnquist
Antonin Scalia
David Hackett Souter
John Paul Stevens
Clarence Thomas

These Judges set the example for promptly acting on motions by doing so in 67 days. Yet, they denied a Mandamus requiring four (4) lower Courts' outstanding motions to remain unanswered, two over one year old.

The Supreme Court in practicing "Bureaucratic Inertia" (a government process where if nothing is done there will be no error) denied the Certiorari, which alternatively confirmed the following:

1. The Federal Rules of Civil Procedure, have been administratively nullified and in particular:

   a. Eliminated the right to a just, speedy and inexpensive determination of every action.

   b. Eliminated a requirement that a judge rule on a motion.

   c. Eliminated such occurrence as "excusable neglect," in not filing an appeal on a timely basis.

   d. Exempted judges from the requirement to answer a motion within 20 days.

e. Allowed the Bankruptcy Courts to ignore due process standards established by Congress.

f. Allowed Bankruptcy Courts with no detailed memorandum of law and no judicially recognized basis, to terminate any litigation in favor of a party that they apparently prefer to see prevail.

2. Eliminated illness as a reason not to fulfill any requirement during an appeal period, which period should not be extended but automatically denied regardless of what his or her condition might be.

3. That it is not a conflict for a Federal Judge to rule on a matter handled by his former law firm.

4. It is permissible for a Federal Judge to remain on the bench even when his bias eliminates his own memory, and impairs his ability to separate fact from fiction.

5. It is permissible and believable for a biased Federal Judge to remarkably determine that numerous national prestigious experienced law firms are all incorrect on every matter that they handle for a specific client.

6. A motion for relief under Rule 60 (b) is no longer available.

7. It is permissible for a court in a Rule 63 filing regarding the inability of a judge to proceed, to make a ruling and not allow the filing party the opportunity to appeal the decision, and furthermore not provide notification until the appeal period has passed.

8. It is permissible for judges on the identical court to seemingly compete to handle cases where they can presumably help friends and hurt entities that they are biased against.

9. Open court biased comments of judges that are recorded are completely permissible and is no indication of bias regardless of their severity or inability on the part of a judge to rule.

10. The Bankruptcy Reform Act of 1978 is invalid.

11. It is permissible for representatives of the trustee in bankruptcy to violate the court's rulings, and not be accountable for mysterious disappearances of assets in their trust, during a period of time when they have the only availability to those assets.

12. It is completely permissible for an officer of the court to withhold and destroy documents, other than Enron's.

13. It is permissible for a federally insured bank to force a sale of the assets of one client to another more favorable client, and for a court to confirm such activity.

14. It is permissible for a court to allow the sale of assets for a low four digit amount, when a reputable law firm is willing, on a completely contingent basis, to prosecute and handle a matter, that it has determined is worth a medium nine digit amount.

15. Irrespective of the fact that three Supreme Court Justices have survived cancer, and one is presently severely afflicted with cancer, petitioners suffering from cancer should not move forward and protect their own position and those of their associates, but preferably lay down and accept whatever transpires.

16. Under 28 U.S.C.§ 455—A judge no longer has to disqualify himself when he admits in open court his bias, and states that he does not understand the facts regarding the matters being heard.

17. A local attorney for a trustee may conspire with a representative of the United States Trustee's office, to satisfy the client that he is representing.

18. It is permissible for a federal bankruptcy court with backing of district court judges to, in effect, enfranchise the district courts judges' former law firm to twist facts and knowingly present falsehoods to a friendly judge not sophisticated to certain transactions, and who admits in open court, on the record, that he does not understand the case.

19. The Supreme Court has a right to deny any citizen's constitutional rights.

Negative Acknowledgments:

The following Senators and Congress persons demonstrated bureaucratic inertia. When contacted, they never responded, nor demonstrated any concern for the losses of 2,484 Creditors (many senior citizens depending on these funds for retirement), nor demonstrated any concern for the denial of funds for cancer research:

Vice President

Dan Quayle (former Senator)

Senators

1. Senator Wayne A. Allard (Colorado)
2. Senator Dennis DeConcini (Retired)
3. Senator Robert Dole (Retired)
4. Senator Russell D. Feingold (Wisconsin)
5. Senator Dianne Feinstein (California)
6. Senator William Philip Gramm (Texas)
7. Senator Chuck Grassley (Iowa)
8. Senator Orrin G. Hatch (Utah)
9. Senator Edward M. Kennedy (Massachusetts)
10. Senator John F. Kerry (Massachusetts)
11. Senator Herbert Kohn (Wisconsin)
12. Senator Jon Kyl (Arizona)
13. Senator Howard M. Metzenbaum (Retired)
14. Senator Barbara A. Mikulski (Maryland)
15. Senator Don Nickles (Oklahoma)
16. Senator Ben Nighthorse-Campbell (Colorado)
17. Senator Charles Schumer (New York)
18. Senator Arlen Specter (Mr.) (Pennsylvania)

19. Senator Strom Thurmond (deceased)

Congress persons

1. Congresswoman Tammy Baldwin (Wisconsin)
2. Congresswoman Helen Delich Bentley (Retired)
3. Congressman Howard L. Berman (California)
4. Congressman Jack Brooks (Retired)
5. Congressman John Conyers, Jr. (Michigan)
6. Congressman Barney Franks (Massachusetts
7. Congressman Mark Green (Wisconsin)
8. Congresswoman Melissa Hart (Pennsylvania)
9. Congressman Joel Hefley (Colorado)
10. Congressman Peter Hoogland (Retired)
11. Congressman Henry Hyde (Illinois)
12. Congresswoman Zoe Lofgren (California)
13. Congressman C. Thomas McMillan (South Carolina)
14. Congresswoman Nancy Pelosi (California)
15. Congressman Mike Pence (Indiana)
16. Congresswoman Linda T. Sanchez (California)
17. Congressman F. James Sensenbrenner, Jr. (Wisconsin)
18. Congressman Lamar Smith (Texas)
19. Congresswoman Maxine Waters (California)

The Foundation thanks the following Federal Bankruptcy Judge for taking the actions that he did, which has allowed the Foundation to disclose publicly what can happen when cancer grows in the Judicial System:

Judge James F. Schneider

Introduction

The Foundation has determined that cancer in any area of the Judicial System appears to equal or exceed that in the human body, and warrants its interest. It is one of 2,484 Creditors, most being senior citizens, to whom the United States Judicial System has denied over $335 million.

The Foundation has analyzed and briefly summarized the facts that appear to have caused this legalized theft to occur.

There are three hundred million people in the United States of America. One hundred million of those people have had cancer, presently have cancer, or will be afflicted with cancer. Cancer terminates the lives of five hundred thousand people in the United States, annually. Notwithstanding the action of the Judicial System, it is universally believed that the Federal government is aware and moving positively to cure this disease.

These 100 million men and women had, in general, the following beliefs:

1. The Federal Senators and Congress persons that are elected will make substantial efforts to protect their constituents.

2. That Federal Judges, who are either appointed for life or elected, will rule justly.

3. The students who study law and become officers of the court, are all honest, do not participate in fraud, conspiracy, bribery, do not destroy documents, nor do they attempt to influence judges.

4. That when an investment or loan is made to a public or private enterprise, the investor is entitled to a return without negative Judiciary interference.

5. When they sign an employment contract, they expect to be compensated per the agreement, and do not expect laws to be warped, aborted and applied to deny them of their income.

6. That when they produce or market a product or perform services, they are entitled to be paid.

7. They do not believe that insurance companies make every effort to avoid claims.

8. They are not aware that bias, envy and jealousy are rampant in certain areas of the judicial system.

9. They did not contemplate that thirty-nine elected officials would turn their backs on them, nor were they aware that some members of the judiciary would develop their own biases and deny their constitutional rights, and that such denial would be confirmed by the Supreme Court of the United States.

10. They were not aware of the bias, envy and jealously amongst some attorneys and other members of the judiciary that destroy companies and individuals for no economic reason.

11. They were not aware that the court system considers a conviction a success, regardless of whether the subject is innocent or guilty, correct or incorrect.

These Creditors selected a relationship with community-oriented owners, officers and directors of companies that they determined were properly managed, and with whom they wanted to participate.

The trust of 2,484 Creditors was destroyed by biased Federal judges, lawyers and influential law firms that those biased judges were formerly partners in. Representation of their wealthy clients immorally denied honest people who believe what is written in the Constitution of the United States of America is practiced. Many small businessmen lost substantial funds, one being forced to go out of business. This is how 2,484 companies and individuals lost over $335 million.

It will never be known how many cancer victims may have never suffered, if the Foundation had received its funds and additional cures for cancer had been developed.

The Supreme Court ruled that judges do not have authority to police prosecutorial misconduct, which leaves convictions in the hands of over zealous prosecutors anxious to get another notch on their guns. The notch is much more worthwhile when they are aware that someone is innocent that they have indicted, than if they are guilty. Furthermore, the Supreme Court ruled that a prosecutor does not have to present any evidence that is favorable to a defendant. It is only necessary to present evidence that will result in an indictment.

The type of actions described above, were addressed on July 4, 1776, in the Declaration of Independence of the Thirteen Colonies. Namely, "whenever any form of government becomes destructive to these ends, it is the right of the people to alter or to abolish it, and to institute new government," or in this case, a new judiciary. "But when a long train of abuses and usurpations, pursuing invariably the same Object evinces a design to reduce them under absolute despotism, it is their right, it is their duty, to throw off such government, and to provide new guards for their future security."

There is a structure, when legislators do not ignore a problem. It is the United States Senate and the House of Representatives, that can amend existing laws to constrain and correct the court system.

The following pages exposes what happened to over two thousand senior citizens when the justice system collapsed in one area, through development of bias, envy, jealousy, influence and misuse of legal procedures.

1

Bias

When an individual rises above the masses, asserts influence, acquires a following, and steps out of the ordinary, he or she incurs the wrath of various individuals with power and authority. This creates negative bias. One incident in one small area demonstrating bias, envy, jealousy, influence and misuse of legal procedures can destroy an entire judicial system.

How does this occur? Lawyers become the cowboys and businessmen become Indians. The cowboys are the graduates of law schools who become prosecutors and destroy businessmen and businesswomen, in some cases warranted and in other cases, unwarranted. Prosecutors should be embarrassed to have generated the bias to prosecute and convict Martha Stewart. There are some good and some bad prosecutions, and the readers of this exposé will have to determine who and what was deserving. Whoever "cowboys" destroy is only a part of the many creditors and investors that suffer along with them, which groups are always forgotten. A successful prosecution only becomes another notch on the gun of the prosecutor, who in turn will present his number of notches, and be employed by an influential law firm that is paid privately to perform similar, but civil injustices.

Judges and many lawyers seem to be able to go to extremes of what is legal and proper and are always excused. This is due to positive bias. Judges hire illegal aliens, do not pay taxes on them, and when denied a position in the federal government, are able to simply disclose the truth and walk away from that infraction. These are the same judges who are supposed to protect the average man, but instead become guilty of exploitation, and go unpunished. Business executives who reach a little too far into the corporate cookie jar, depending on who they are, and what their connections are, and who they go hunting with, can end up walking away.

If the President of General Electric had never been involved in a contested divorce, the General Electric shareholders would have never known what his perks and retirement benefits were. This is the same General Electric that owns insurance companies that legally avoid claims that do not equal the hundreds of millions of dollars paid (given) to their former chairman and other executives.

Many prosecutions, indictments, and bureaucratic harassments are first generated by bias, and then the misuses of legal procedures become weapons.

The Don'ts of Generating Negative Bias:

1. Don't become so ill that you are unable to protect your associates and self.
2. Don't be successful, particularly if you started with nothing.
3. Don't be a minority.
4. Don't be vocal.
5. Don't be litigious.

6. Don't display individuality.
7. Don't be too tall, too short, too fat, too thin, too dark, too light or too plain.
8. Do not allow yourself to be in positions where you may be honored, be it for good deeds or purely fund raising.
9. Don't be a celebrity, or gain recognition, or be well known.
10. Don't be rich.
11. Don't participate in publicly beneficial activities.
12. Don't be a leader.
13. Don't be religious or an agnostic.
14. Don't assert influence in any form.
15. Don't openly expect protection that the Constitution of the United States guarantees to you.

If one fits into any of the above categories, bias may be generated by someone in the judiciary.

Displays of Negative Bias:

1. A judge prevents the results of any test showing complete innocence, from being presented to a grand jury.
2. A judge opens a case by relaying his opinion of what a decision should be, before a hearing.
3. A judge ends a case by influencing a jury's decision.
4. A judge prevents a lawyer from properly presenting all facts and matters.
5. A judge becomes so incensed that he issues a ridiculous decision, is reversed on appeal but remains on the bench.
6. An FBI agent informs a federal prosecutor that the defendant subpoenaed as a witness in litigation, another FBI agent.

7. Members of a federal agency specifically investigate members of a specific religion.
8. An appeals court justice refuses to recuse himself after representing an adverse party in a dispute.
9. A judge creates rules to prevent a successful law firm from representing a client.
10. The Justice Department determines that a certain party is not guilty, but because of who he is, decides to bring an action anyway—selective prosecution.
11. A major law firm that gave advice in a major transaction, was found incorrect, but a judge dismissed the case because of who was damaged.
12. One manufacturer is indicted, while a wealthy neighboring manufacturer of the same product, equally as culpable is not indicted.
13. A Judge receives telephone calls or has meetings, exparté with non-involved interested parties.
14. The Office of Professional Responsibility (OPR) looks through tinted glasses and cannot see any evidence of misconduct, in spite of how obvious the evidence may be.
15. An East Coast company is unable to have a fair arbitration on the West Coast.
16. A judge schedules hearings without notification to all parties.

The above is a mere sampling of the bias that denied 2,484 Creditors their proper day in court.

Positive Bias[1] is the act(s) of the judiciary allowing certain individuals to violate normal legal procedures, and not be criticized or accused of any wrongdoing.

---

1.   The most publicized example was that no action was taken against the former President of General Electric, who evidently can do no wrong.

2

Jealousy and Envy

The "infected" judiciary is comprised of people, most of whom have had no experience other than going to law school, practicing law, and usually are not exposed to other more mundane experiences. They do not create a product, sell a product, meet a payroll, file a financial statement, or exert themselves physically.

There are legal graduates that become court clerks, magistrates, and in some cases with no experience whatsoever, end up being federal judges.

They watch the world go by. They see businesses being built, individuals becoming successful in various fields of endeavor other than the law, and they represent them in documentation and arguments, but do not receive the same financial benefits and easily become envious and jealous of accomplishments and compensation.

They become aware of individuals who start with nothing, and build billion-dollar companies. Their only accomplishment is relegated to helping a client build further, or find ways to criticize and tear down what others accomplish. This is the basic manifestation of jealousy and envy, which can occur on a limited basis, but can expand and cause substantial damage.

The people with accomplishments have opportunities to lead charitable organizations. They raise funds for many community projects through their many contacts that are developed in their endeavors. The legal profession usually does not have the opportunity to enjoy these endeavors or be as exposed to these opportunities.

The legal profession observes people who are successful in all challenges of life, and prevail in disputes.

They observe growing companies that make multiple acquisitions in short periods of time, and are written up in business magazines. They observe banks lending these companies large sums of money. What they receive are "crumbs" in drawing up the papers for those transactions, which crumbs irritate the wounds of jealousy and envy.

Employees of various governmental agencies, enjoy working together, when the opportunity arises, to help destroy the people that we will call the "haves."

The justice system, when a cancer develops, separates the world into haves and have-nots. Most members of the judicial system are have-nots. Some become very wealthy, but never with pride of creation, but more so, with pride of destruction.

The success of the businesses that 2,484 people invested in, sold to, bought from, loaned to, and admired, was hurt by the legal tools mis-applied by the have-nots.

3

Influence

The legal community influences each other, often to the detriment of the rest of the population. However, they object to the influence that the rest of the population develops, along with their bias, jealousy and envy.

Executives and bankers donate to the campaigns of various politicians. They influence the politicians that they donate to.

There are business organizations that give the various members the opportunity to know more about each other, their businesses, their problems, and in many cases those problems are with lawyers and governmental agencies.

Some corporate executives might have had tenure in various governmental agencies, such as the Federal Bureau of Investigation, the Treasury Department, the Federal Trade Commission, the Securities and Exchange Commission and many more. People meet and influence other people.

The Citizens Foundation for a Cancer Free America, Inc. (Foundation), learned that its major benefactor personally knew the former deputy director of the Federal Bureau of Investigation, leading investment bankers, Senators, Congressmen, their families, several generals, several admirals, other executives of billion dollar companies. He also knows bank presidents, and former bank presidents and college presidents.

People that circulate outside of the legal community, develop many contacts, and from time to time, will contact those people in influential positions to help them or to offer help.

There is a world of thousands of contacts outside of the legal community. They meet doctors and help those doctors raise funds for many medical endeavors, such as Invitro fertilization, cures for various types of cancer, and heart disease.

This exposé will describe some examples of efforts to influence persons of authority, which caused 2,484 people to lose $335 million.

4

Litigation

The judiciary, in some areas, demonstrates prejudice against individuals who have been cast into litigation for whatever reason, in spite of the legal fees it generates.

With more lawyers, there will be more litigation, and with more laws, there will be more criminals.

Notwithstanding, litigation touches and invades the sanctum of the judiciary. The accidental knowledge that an FBI agent on a sting operation, was not only attempting to implicate the Balistrieri family of Greenfield, Wisconsin, but was also busy entertaining "desperate housewives," upset the judicial community. The sting operation is described in a book called Donnie Brasco, which eventually became a movie. The former deputy director of the FBI arranged for the socially minded FBI agent to be deposed in a child custody matter. The Justice Department found this use of influence completely unsatisfactory, yet it was necessary in litigation.

Time and time again the Securities and Exchange Commission will investigate a relatively small company, costing the shareholders millions of dollars, and after months of incurring expenses not only for the government, but for the company's shareholders, notify the company in writing that there had been no violation of the Securities Laws.

One does not have to go to Australia, to observe kangaroo courts. They can be observed in Baltimore, Norfolk, and in Richmond. It is unnecessary to cross an ocean. If one has been in litigation, every piece of litigation thereafter, will be mentioned in any future litigation and create an aura that there is something wrong with litigation that has been specifically allowed by Congress in the form of 86 Federal Rules of Civil Procedure, which the Supreme Court wishes to remove from the rights of citizens.

For example, one appeals court judge refused to recuse himself for having represented an involved party while practicing law, but another judge on the same appeals court recused himself because his grandchild owned 100 shares in a trust, which was a minimal part of the millions outstanding, of the involved entity.

When a governmental agency is prosecuting a case, it changes the rules. It will send a Martha Stewart to jail for something no more serious than privately urinating on a sidewalk before a rain storm, but themselves will allow the withholding of documents, destruction of documents, changing dates of occurrences, and force people to testify and perjure themselves to confirm the changes the government needs to win a case. But when an appeal or an objection is presented in court, the government and the supposedly independent judges overseeing fairness band together to the detriment of the defendant.

It has been publicly stated that the attorney, Roy Cohn, when he was working for Senator McCarthy, had expartè conversations with the judge in the Julius and Ethel Rosenberg case which ended up in their execution. Lawyers with knowledge of that have practiced the same methods that Roy Cohn used, and when such accusations of these illegal practices are made, the Office of Professional Responsibility (OPR) that oversees this type of infraction looks the other way, and passes out halos.

If a polygraph test or a DNA sample will prove someone innocent, or correct, there are armies of judges and lawyers that will attempt to prove and create law to make the tests invalid.

There is a Senate Judiciary Committee, a House Judiciary Committee, an OPR per the above, Canons of Legal Ethics,[1] Attorney Grievance Commissions, Attorney Generals and U.S. Attorneys, all of whom offer little to no protection from judicial infractions.

The summary is that all of these supposed checks are only to protect lawyers, and no one else. Had these checks been properly applied, 2,484 entities would not have lost $335 million.

---

1.   Melvin Hirschman is Bar Counsel at the Attorney Grievance Commission of Maryland. During a recent five year period, the commission reviewed 9.561 complaints and only determined that 103 (1.077 percent) should be sanctioned.

5

Misuse of Legal Procedures

The 75th Congress of the United States of America approved the "Federal Rules of Civil Procedure. The 86 Rules took effect on September 1, 1938. They were to govern all civil proceedings in actions brought after they took effect.

Amendments were adopted by the Supreme Court on December 27, 1946, December 29, 1948, April 17, 1961, and January 21, 1963, further clarifying and confirming the Rules.

None of those amendments eliminated the Federal Rules of Civil Procedure, nor did they change the very basic principle, which is described in Rule 1, Scope and Purpose of Rules as follows: These rules govern the procedure in the United States district courts in all suits of a civil nature whether cognizable as cases at law or in equity or in admiralty, with the exceptions stated in Rule 81. They shall be construed and administered to secure the <u>just</u>, <u>speedy</u>, and <u>inexpensive</u> determination of every action.

The justices of the present Supreme Court, many district court judges, and lawyers practicing before those various courts, have directly or indirectly attempted to eliminate what the 75th Congress of the United States approved as the law of the land.

There are some judges and lawyers who make a career out of violating and ignoring these Federal Rules, destroying the entire judicial system. This exposé in no way can describe every infraction, in that they are too voluminous. The Foundation is trying to prevent and cure cancer in at least one hundred million United States inhabitants. Included are a Supreme Court justice who is presently suffering from cancer, and three Supreme Court justices who might have been somewhat cured, and should be aware of the following infractions in one small area that has denied the Foundation to date, $75 million:

1. In late December 2004, the Supreme Court of the United States denied a Petition for a Writ of Certiorari only requesting that four outstanding motions be answered, one outstanding for 460 days, one for 432 days, one for 320 days, and the last for 265 days. The Supreme Court was not being asked to make decisions regarding the context of the motions, but only that the motions be answered, which would guarantee the requirements under Rule 1, namely a speedy determination of every action.

2. The Supreme Court, left-handedly, set an example by denying the motion in 67 days, but took no action in the dilatory and illegal behavior of the lower courts.

3. The Supreme Court in its position, negated the 86 Federal Rules of Civil Procedure, which they should be upholding.

4. The court systems in demonstrating their bias, jealousy and envy, against one individual or group, ignores the damage done to hundreds of thousands of others. Although Martha Stewart's

company's stock has recovered, the shareholders who sold their stock at a loss have been severely damaged and will not be compensated.

5. In spite of good applicable law, the court system avoids the term "excusable neglect" when it involves the extension of time for an appeal. There is little concern if a lawyer or client cannot be available under certain circumstances. Yet, Justice William H. Rehnquist has recognized illness himself, by not voting on certain matters that he was not familiar with. Again, examples are displayed but not enforced

6. Large law firms, in spite of Rule 11, are allowed to paper opponents and misstate facts, thus making it difficult in many cases for injured parties to obtain proper results. This practice avoids the Federal Rules of Civil Procedure, 1, regarding speedy and inexpensive determination of every action.

7. When a judge is the individual responsible to answer a motion within 20 days, for example in the case of a recusal motion, and he does not, he is not considered to have violated the Federal Rules of Civil Procedure.

8. Many judges are placed in a position to rule on matters that are represented by their former law partners, and do not recuse themselves as required to avoid any appearance of bias. In too many instances, they do rule, and often in favor of those matters handled by former partners.

9. Judges will change dates of hearings without notifying all involved parties.

10. With a friendly judge, a law firm with close ties to that judge, can create a completely fictional story and have it believed by the judge, who does not want to hear what attorneys from other areas might state. Sanctions are too often issued as threats, when the court believes a matter is not proceeding the way it wishes to see it determined.

11. Courts sit back, and unless there is a prime example such as Enron, documents are withheld and destroyed with full knowledge of the court, which takes no corrective measures.

12. Much expert testimony is nothing other than a fraud on the court system.

13. Protective orders are usually awarded to friends of the court. There is no exclusion in the Federal Rules of Civil Procedure for actions of biased judges.

14. "Finding of facts" in an unfriendly courtroom are often findings of "fiction."

15. Honest judges recuse themselves per the rules when certain circumstances exist. Notwithstanding, too many judges who should not proceed, due to bias or lack of knowledge or lack of understanding, improperly proceed.

16. Some Bankruptcy judges continually violate the Federal Rules of Civil Procedure with no sanctions against them.

17. Lawyers "misstate" facts and are outnumbered by the lawyers that warp facts, and then judges in some districts improperly find the warped facts to be correct.

18. Many individuals and corporations retain experienced and expensive lawyers to draft documents and give advice. It is remarkable when a judge finds such advice and documents to be incorrect, and the attorney has no liability.

19. Judges accept expartè telephone calls during litigation, with no retribution.

20. The "old boys' network" between judges and lawyers make phone calls and receive phone calls with the attitude, "you just cannot let this happen," even though it may be a proper decision.

21. Prosecutions and decisions are based on bias, envy, jealousy, past litigation and possible influence.

The worse infraction of the Judicial System is Selective Prosecution. The Foundation is overwhelmed by the weaknesses of our Judicial System that has been displayed. Selective Prosecution is a procedure used to determine who may violate the laws, and who may not, and who should be a statistic (even though innocent) and who should not. Had H.R.4079 been passed, Judge Allen Ginsburg (who during his Supreme Court nomination hearings admitted to using marijuana at College), and President Bill Clinton (who did not inhale) would both be under the jurisdiction of the Federal Bureau of Prisons. Many other public officials who have admitted drug usage would be with them. None of these officials were selected or indicted, but Mayor Marion Barry, Jr. of Washington, DC was "selected," indicted, convicted and incarcerated. Norman Sisisky, the deceased congressman from Virginia, plead his former Company in Petersburg, Virginia guilty of price-fixing, and his company paid the fine. He, of course, was not indicted. It helps to be a congressman and not be "selected."

Former Attorney General William Barr was very ecstatic when the first President Bush nominated him for that position. He found that it was not necessary to indict Republican Governor Bob Martinez of Florida for donating sixty-three thousand dollars to the Florida Republicans. He found no "criminal intent" and Governor Martinez was named to be the drug director.

President Bush's brother, John Ellis Bush (Jeb) the Florida Governor, was involved in a loan that cost Broward Federal Savings and Loan Association of Sunrise, Florida $4,970,000. Suits were filed, but Jeb was excluded. There was no known investigation. Another brother of the President, Neil, was involved in the Silverado Savings & Loan Association and paid a fine of $50,000. The Silverado failure cost the government $1 billion. When President Bush sold stock of Harken Oil, he had insider information about its financials in that he was on the Board of Directors, and yet he was not indicted. While Neil had his wrist slapped, Charles Keating of Lincoln Savings of Irvine, California stood in the courtroom, selected and shackled to his son, requesting a bail bond.

The above examples describe an unjust system, operated by some dishonest judges and lawyers, pandering to influential people to the detriment of those who are not in the inner circle.

Most judges and lawyers are reputable. However, when they assert what is correct and legal, they often injure their own ability in the future to deal with courts, and other lawyers and law firms.

There may be more infractions of the legal system than there are varieties of cancer, which indicates the immediate need for legislation to correct a sick system. One cancer can multiply and appear in other areas.

There are tools and rules that have been well established, Canons of Legal Ethics describing proper behavior of attorneys, OPR, grievance committees, Attorney Generals, but without one "stout-hearted man or woman" who will stand up for what is right and what was originally expected by the 75th Congress, these checks and balances are a dream.

Notwithstanding, it is not a dream that 2,484 people lost $335 million, because those responsible individuals have not operated a clean judicial system throughout the country.

6

Results Of A Damaged Judiciary

The Foundation, similar to other charitable organizations is, very protective of its benefactors. The Foundation through its own efforts, has researched, reviewed, investigated and analyzed why they, and one hundred million cancer patients, were denied $75 million for research.

The Foundation reviewed what happened to one benefactor, to understand how and why cancer grows in the judicial system.

Voluminous files have been reviewed, and in particular, those incidences that caused their major benefactor, and thus themselves, to be denied their funds as well as their constitutional rights.

The denial fits within the Bias, Jealousy, Envy, Litigation, Influence, and Misuse of Legal Procedures all directed at one individual, because he fit within the target perceived by one area of the Judicial System. The System always ignores the damage it does to innocent bystanders. The Foundation has described in one word what happened—Cancer.

To respect the privacy of the benefactor, he will be referred to as "X," his companies as "A" and his competitor as "C."

X survived the most severe type of physical cancer, to only be infected by the judicial cancer while he was recovering. Today, the Foundation is convinced that X recovered in order to cure the judicial cancer, as he overcame the physical cancer.

X was a prime target who attracted the five weapons of the local judiciary. X had started a company with a small bank loan, and at the end of 1985, A had revenues of $1.2 billion, 41,000 employees, and was doing business in 43 states plus the District of Columbia, Canada, and England. A operated in ten different fields of endeavor.

A was built by growing its core business and by acquiring many other companies, including 32 different businesses purchased throughout the United States, over the short period of 30 months. Thus, X's publicity attracted envy and jealousy.

X always found time for community projects such as operating an organization that fought all types of prejudice including religious, color, race, gender, and physical appearance. X was on television on a daily basis, asking anyone who believed that he or she had been a victim of any type of prejudice, to contact X, and many injured parties were helped. X furthermore participated in fund raising for many charities, including several religious organizations, two hospitals, two colleges, two secondary schools, and the Boy Scouts of America. X was certainly conspicuous in his activities, and obviously drew attention from those that would like to tear down his commendable efforts. He always made time to help others.

X was involved in a divorce and custody action, and was awarded custody. Part of the litigation required the aid of the former Deputy Director of the FBI that X knew personally, to help locate an FBI agent who was needed to testify. The agent was made available. The judiciary does not like influence as X used it.

While protecting a minority investment banker from prejudice, X incurred the wrath of the Securities and Exchange Commission (SEC) which began harassing A's many operations.

A made an unfriendly tender offer for a large customer of one of its subsidiaries, which in its own defense brought a lawsuit in Federal District Court, alleging violations of the Williams Act. The judge determined that there was no violation of that Act. Notwithstanding, the SEC, wanting to harass A, questioned the judge's decision, and commenced its own six-month investigation, which cost A's shareholders hundreds of thousands of dollars. After six months of wasted time and money, the SEC wrote to A with notification that there had been no violation of the securities laws in the unfriendly takeover.

A continued to make marketing history, and one major competitor, C, commenced a program of predatory pricing, namely, illegally selling products under their actual costs. A's New York law firm brought an action on its behalf against its Southern competitor, C, for violating the laws governing Restraint of Trade. The Norfolk,

Virginia courthouse was not a friendly place to be, and when A's attorney attempted to describe what competition was trying to accomplish, he was told that if he mentioned the name of the president of the defendant company, C again, that he would be held in contempt. The case was lost, but the competitor temporarily ceased predatory pricing.

Notwithstanding, X had incurred the wrath of a major competitor with strong political influence. X specifically instructed his organization to have no contacts with its competitors, and A enforced its antitrust compliance program. X noted that a neighboring company was selling the same product with the same competition at substantially higher prices, indicating pricing arrangements.

The adverse predatory pricing decision was appealed, in the Richmond, Virginia Fourth Circuit Federal Court of Appeals. The presiding judge refused to recuse himself in spite of his prior relationship with parties adverse to A. The predatory pricing appeal was denied.

The damage was done. There appeared to be much pressure on the Judiciary from C's home office in the Southeastern part of the country to bring some type of action against X and A, which ended up implicating C as well. It happened in the form of an antitrust action alleging price-fixing. The Justice Department was eager to cooperate in that they just lost an argument to destroy the entire franchise system that both A and C participated in.

The Justice Department felt that they had an open and shut case, and alleged that the president of C's subsidiary company and a vice president of A met in Ocean City, Maryland at a convention in 1983 to discuss price-fixing. The government's case did not stand up because the president of C's subsidiary was in Chicago at that time, but the government had no problem intimidating witnesses who would perjure themselves and testify that such meeting really happened in 1982, while the predatory pricing appeal was still outstanding, with no actual proof whatsoever that the two individuals had ever met in Ocean City or discussed price-fixing. In 1982, there was no predatory pricing by C.

A retained Williams & Connolly of Washington, DC, the law firm that Brendan Sullivan, (who had successfully represented Oliver North in the Iran Contra affair) was a partner in. When the Federal judge, officiating in the case, learned of the representation, he ruled that it would be a conflict if Williams & Connolly represented X, in that they were handling the investigation on behalf of A as to whether C had started predatory pricing a second time. This necessitated quickly finding another law firm.

In 1983 (not 1982), unbeknownst to X, certain of A's employees had conversations with employees of C, regarding violations of the Robinson/Patman Act, but not fixing prices. A retained a second Washington law firm to take over the case, Miller, Cassidy, Larroca & Lewin ("Miller") which was frightened away by the same judge during the Grand Jury phase. In August 1987, X submitted to a polygraph test administered by Raymond Weir, Jr. (used by NSA for over a decade), which results showed his having no knowledge or participation in price-fixing. The FBI and Justice Department took the position that Weir did not administer a proper polygraph test, and refused to submit it, or other exculpatory information to the Grand Jury. The Miller law firm argued that the polygraph results properly should be presented to the Grand Jury. The presiding judge refused and commented "that everyone knew that X was guilty, anyway." The Miller firm filed an appeal, and the judge arranged to bring down an indictment before the appeal could be heard.

In 1985, an attorney who was a prime example of being affected by bias, envy and jealousy returned to the United States from overseas. His former law firm represented X's family for many years. His sister was the maid of honor at X's wedding. The attorney was Lawrence I. Weisman ("Weisman"). In addition to the above, Weisman was the son of X's parents' best friends. Weisman suggested that they take their fathers to lunch, which they did. Weisman was a Harvard Law School graduate, had represented many large companies but unknown to X, had become very involved with Roy Cohn and such individuals as Tom Boland and Neil Walsh all described in a book called <u>Citizen Cohn</u>. After lunch, Weisman, who had represented X in 1956, joined X at his offices, and offered his "help" in all business matters. X accepted, having known him for years.

In 1984, the Justice Department began an investigation of A regarding price-fixing in two Southern areas. A believed that the investigation was of the predatory pricing practices of C, and directed the Williams & Connolly law firm representing his company to cooperate with the government completely.

In 1985, A sold the subsidiary that had experienced the predatory pricing problem for $160 million, not aware of the direction of the Justice Department's investigation. X even gave a $5 million personal guarantee to the purchaser to cover antitrust litigation that he did not believe existed. A then purchased a major foodservice company for $225 million. It was merged with A's existing food operations.

In March of 1986, a class action was filed against A based on its not meeting projections. A did not know that Weisman was behind the action.

Later in 1986, Weisman conceived a plan, which was later admitted by Weisman's own affidavit in 1991, his sixth wife's affidavit, Justice Department and FBI documents, and testimony of other participants. The plan was to weaken X and A, manipulate government agencies, join with others such as the Harry and Jeannette Weinberg Foundation, a client of Weisman's, in insider trading of A's securities, purchase such securities at a discount, and "greenmail" a settlement by having A purchase securities at par. Weisman attempted a similar program against Plains Resources, a firm headed by a former brother-in-law, a member of the Mellon family of Pittsburgh, Pennsylvania.

In late July 1987, Weisman was deposed by the SEC regarding insider trading of Arundel Corporation stock, and launched into a long conversation regarding A and X. It was later learned that the

SEC attorney passed all of Weisman's comments on to the Justice Department.

In February of 1988, the SEC, based on Weisman's allegations and comments, began a formal investigation of A and X. A incurred substantial legal fees. The SEC announced in 1990 that no infractions were discovered and terminated the investigation.

While the SEC was considering proceeding with an investigation of A, the Justice Department sent a "Target Letter" to X and A, based on information provided by the SEC from Weisman's conversation.

In July 1987, Weisman attended a defense session supposedly representing A and X, at the Williams & Connolly law firm. He immediately reported the strategy to Neil Walsh, a paid FBI informant, and friend of the infamous late attorney, Roy Cohn.

X, A, and its third defense law firm headed by Robert Morse met with four members of the Justice Department, presented the polygraph test, and discussed the entire matter. Approximately ten days thereafter, one member of the Justice Department called Mr. Morse and told him that the Justice Department had spent more time on X than any other potential defendant and felt that it was a "seesaw," but they were going to indict and let the jury decide.

Alan Dershowitz, the well known Harvard Law School Professor, stated that "This is the weakest case I have ever seen the Justice Department bring in my entire career, based as it is on uncorroborated testimony of a bought witness that was himself disputed by another government witness." It is a shoo-in for a government prosecutor to secure an indictment and conviction of a Jewish businessman if it is brought in the Norfolk, Virginia, Federal District Court.

In November 1987, while Weisman was recovering from an appendectomy, two Justice Department attorneys visited him in the hospital.

Also in December 1987, A sold its major subsidiary, doing approximately $1 billion in annual revenues, to a leveraged buyout fund for $450 million with the assumption of $105 million in publicly held debentures. The trustee of the debenture issue had no problem with issuing an amendment relieving A of interest and principal on the debentures. Then, at Weisman's and his client, the Weinberg Foundation's instigation, the trustee received three letters, one from the Union Bank of Switzerland, one from Salomon Brothers, and the other from Fidelity Management objecting to the trustee's position that there was no problem. The Indenture Trustee was later replaced by a firm friendly to the three investment firms.

The compelling reason for the sale of the subsidiary, was the amount of volume that the subsidiary of A was doing with various governmental agencies, and should X be convicted, that business could have been lost. X had fear of conviction in view of his poor and shocking experience in the Norfolk, Virginia federal courthouse several years prior, when an action was brought for predatory pricing.

In March 1988, the Justice Department attorneys were reminded by an FBI agent of the incident when X deposed an FBI agent in a child custody matter.

On April 3, 1988, the trial of X began. The judge opened the trial by stating "will the guilty parties, I mean the accused parties, please stand." Weisman, prior to and during the trial continued his contact with the SEC, FBI, Justice Department and made direct phone calls to the presiding judge, something he learned from Roy Cohn.

Prior to this trial, the Richmond manager of A's subsidiary, was found guilty. It was reported in newspapers that the judge was urging the government to seek further indictments of higher executives. The judge's continual comments were unbelievable. The trial judge assumed the role of an active prosecutor, rather than an evenhanded overseer.

The subsidiary of C pled guilty and paid a substantial fine, which led the judge to believe that the guilty plea proved a threshold issue against all defendants. The judge several times during the trial, stated that he believed that both the C subsidiary president and X, were guilty. The judge stated in open court, "I am having trouble separating one from the other." The judge embarked upon a systematic course of conduct designed to ensure that the jury would reach a conclusion he had reached long before the trial began, that all defendants were guilty.

The judge's attitude toward the government changing the entire story from 1983 to 1982 was "ladies and gentlemen of the jury you can consider it changed if you want." When defense counsel sought to undermine a government witness's credibility, the judge interrupted with the following comment "the witness is not on trial here on this day at this time and in this place. Who is on trial here are these defendants." The judge conducted a continual circus atmosphere during the entire trial and the non-sophistication of the jury in antitrust matters, resulted in findings of guilt.

This was a one-witness case with no guilt documentation of X. All government and defense witnesses contradicted the one witness who had plea-bargained, and none corroborated the witness. The witness that plea-bargained changed the date of the beginning of the alleged conspiracy to one year earlier, namely in 1982, because the president of the C subsidiary, was not where the government alleged him to be in 1983.

Similar charges were not brought against neighboring manufacturers of the same product, some of whom pled guilty. According to a leak from the Antitrust Division of the Justice Department, a neighboring manufacturer provided information that led directly to the indictments of A and C's subsidiary president. The prior Sunday night broadcast of "60 Minutes" regarding price-fixing in the industry, was rerun during the second week of the trial, similar to the programs run prior to Martha Stewart's trial. The FBI attempted to have X's former wife testify as an adverse witness.

After six weeks of the trial, the judge turned to the jury and said, "well I have made up my mind, and now it is your turn." This is the same judge who refused to have the polygraph turned over to the Grand Jury, and stated in open court that "everyone knew that X was guilty." On May 16, 1988, X was convicted and later served five months in prison.

Both an appeal to the Fourth Circuit regarding X's conviction and the Writ of Certiorari to the Supreme Court were denied. The judge's comments in the opening, during and at the closing of the six-week trial meant nothing to either court. It was permissible to create a circus atmosphere during the six-week trial. It was evidently acceptable that the judge received telephone calls from Weisman, and even went as far as excusing himself from the courtroom to take a Weisman call.

After one confirmed call that lasted for five minutes, the Judge stormed back into the courtroom and called an attorney of X, who is now a Federal Appeal's Court Judge, on the telephone in open court. The appeal decision did not consider that it was a one-witness case, and that there was only one plea-bargained witness, with no corroboration.

The government presented a new "vicarious liability" theory, in that because X was chairman, he should be guilty. Neither Appeals Court cared, although no such legal theory existed. They reversed the judge, when he wanted to physically lock up the company by padlocking the doors. He was reversed on the unprecedented out-landish ruling, but allowed to stay on the bench.

The judge made numerous contempt threats to attorneys representing X, A and the C subsidiary's President. The judge made it impossible to properly present a defense. The one government witness who testified to price-fixing continually turned to the Justice Department lawyers looking for affirmation of each lie he told.

After the finding of X's and A's guilt, the various Circuits jumped in for the kill. The Eighth Federal District Court ruled that A was jointly and severely liable for principal and interest on publicly held debentures assigned to the purchaser of another major subsidiary, even though the Indenture Trustee had allowed the transaction. Such decision was rendered only after three investment banking firms asserted their influence and objected. The transaction of the sale of A's large subsidiary was handled based on the opinion of a major Cleveland, Ohio law firm who was ruled not liable for faulty advice.

In early August 1988, X's counsel wrote a letter to the OPR regarding charges of prosecutorial misconduct. An additional letter was written to the Justice Department on August 12, 1988, when it was learned that Weisman was in conversations not only with the FBI and the Justice Department, but the judge as well who was presiding in the Antitrust trial. Phone records were obtained proving the judge's conversations with Weisman, and neither the OPR or the Justice Department did anything. Investigations were drawn out until various Attorney Generals were replaced. Their replacements did nothing.

Amidst the Justice Department's actions, X's being sentenced to five months in prison, lawyers' opinions being reversed by courts, in February 1992, the Department of Justice advised that their second full review had been completed. The conduct of the Department of Justice was found completely proper in spite of the vast evidence produced to the contrary. Both Appeals filings were unsuccessful. The Judicial System was ready to bury X.

Notwithstanding, in 1988 a Federal District Court ruled that Weisman was overwhelmingly found to have represented X and A, and sanctioned for violating attorney-client privilege, proving that the Judicial System does properly function in some areas.

The Justice Department displays a knack of selecting questionable informants. When Weisman arrived back in the United States, he was with his sixth wife. By the time he was sanctioned, he was in the process of getting divorced and marrying a seventh time. He followed Roy Cohn's example of expartè conversations with judges. He died in 1988, in the apartment of his male lover; while on the telephone to Switzerland talking to potential wife number seven. The autopsy performed determined that he died of AIDS.

Amongst overwhelming odds and pressures, on June 1, 1992 A filed a prepackaged bankruptcy plan. In reviewing all documents, it was discovered that Irvin Walker, a partner in the law firm of Miles & Stockbridge was attorney to the Creditors committee.

During the reorganization and cleaning up the bankruptcy loose ends, and a redirection of A's efforts for acquisitions, X's health began to wane. He physically slowed down. X and his house counsel traveled to Seattle, Washington to negotiate an acquisition shortly before Christmas in 1995. During the meeting, X suffered two grand mal seizures. The cause of the seizures was misdiagnosed for over two years. During X's illness, executives of A proceeded with its business plan and employed reputable and highly experienced attorneys for advice and documentation. Other than being consulted and driven to occasional meetings, X was incapacitated from December 1995 through early 2002.

Two major law firms, Miles & Stockbridge and Venable, Baetjer and Howard, LLP, with the acquiescence of Federal Bankruptcy Judge James F. Schneider, preyed on the situation. In August 1996, A purchased Winterland Concessions, a screen printing and promotional company located in California, owned by Music Corporation of America (MCA), the Seagram subsidiary. With a $23 million six-month bridge loan from Cerberus Partners and Gordon Brothers Capital, A consummated the acquisition. In spite of the comfort letter to the contrary from MCA, in less than two months it was determined that MCA collected certain accounts receivable that they warranted were still on the Winterland books. The bridge loan was in default the day of its consummation. The deficiency was unsuccessfully arbitrated. It was later learned that the lead arbitrator was with the firm that represented MCA. The two lenders were completely uncooperative.

During the settlement of the Winterland acquisition in 1996, with advice from Piper & Marbury (now Piper Rudnick), a large national law firm, A arranged for Winterland to purchase all the assets of one of A's own subsidiaries that was a screen printer, and to lease from it certain other assets, for $14 million. Seven million dollars of those lease payments were earmarked to repay publicly held A debentures, most of which are owned by 2,000 senior citizens or their heirs.

The two lenders of the bridge loan were represented by Miles & Stockbridge, which, based on its representation of the Creditors committee of A in 1992, was not only a severe conflict, but Miles worked adversely to the interests of the A Creditors committee. In addition, Miles later became local counsel to an Illinois bank in an action adverse to A, thus participating in three conflicts.

The two lenders bribed the chief financial officer of the MCA subsidiary, who admitted to the bribe and caused the six-month bridge loan not to be refinanced. In 1997, as obviously part of their plan, the two lenders forced A to sell its stock in Winterland to the lenders, with certain concessions that were given to A for a one year period. Three months later, the two lenders placed Winterland in bankruptcy. Its only default was not repaying the remainder of the loan to its new owners, the two lenders. A reduced the loan from $23 million to $13 million during the six months it owned the company. Federal Bankruptcy Judge Schneider later characterized this period and amazing pay down of $10 million as "mismanagement." All of the obligations agreed to for the one-year period were eliminated through bankruptcy, which is not why the bankruptcy laws were created. This caused a domino effect on all of the related subsidiaries of A, costing 2,484 people over $335 million.

A's counsel filed an action against the two lenders in 1997, which hearing was belatedly set to be heard on October 6, 1999, before Federal Bankruptcy Judge Schneider. Three months prior to that date, the Indenture trustee for the 2,000 debenture holders that were owed over $7 million, through its attorney, Venable, Baetjer and Howard, LLP, one of the cooperative attorneys described above, filed an action against X and others. Venable had committed a severe error in forcing one of A's subsidiaries into bankruptcy, thus disenfranchising the 2,000 debenture holders.

During X's illness and recovery, Venable, Baetjer and Howard, LLP, apparently to cover its own error, brought the action against X, alleging a series of fictional occurrences, not worth describing the details of in this summary, which was filed before the same acquiescing Bankruptcy Judge Schneider, who himself had never practiced law. During this total period of time X was ill, A was being operated by its other executives, and X was unaware of most of the details.

In March 1998, X was properly diagnosed with pancreatic cancer, operated on, treated, and given a short period of time to live. He was one of fourteen volunteers that agreed to participate in an experimental immunization program, and was one of only three volunteers who survived. X was severely wounded, and the Judicial System took complete advantage and attempted to destroy him.

The Federal Bankruptcy Judge Schneider dismissed A's lawsuit against the two lenders, cooperated with the attorneys representing the trustee of the $7 million debenture issue, allowed the subsidiary of A to be forced into bankruptcy thus disenfranchising the debenture holders, and appointed a Chapter 7 bankruptcy trustee who depended on such appointments from the judge to earn her living. She refused to allow an appeal to the judge's decision, which A's attorney wanted to bring.

During X's illness, the president of another A subsidiary in Illinois, inflated its inventory, thus placing a recent loan from LaSalle Business Credit in default. LaSalle Business Credit is a subsidiary of LaSalle Bank of Chicago, which in turn is owned by a Netherlands bank, ABN Amro.

One of X's sons, took over the responsibilities of the Illinois subsidiary, during his father's illness, and attempted to work with LaSalle Business Credit, to no avail. He arranged for his family to invest substantial additional funds in the Illinois subsidiary, all of which LaSalle Business Credit usurped by increasing interest rates and charging excessive fees.

X's son experienced severe and unreasonable prejudice, in his dealing with a female vice president, which LaSalle was aware of and appeared to approve of her misbehavior. With minimum experience, he replaced the entire management team and made great progress in correcting the problems. He arranged a $70 million financing for the Illinois subsidiary to purchase a customer for $50 million, repay LaSalle Business Credit fully, and investment bankers involved believed that the stock of A's subsidiary in Illinois, with the refinancing and acquisition, would be worth $150 million. Half of that amount, or $75 million, was committed to fight cancer.

There were constant problems with LaSalle Business Credit. In early December 2000, they insisted that the Illinois subsidiary sell all of its assets to another client of the bank, and eliminate the $4 million due the Illinois subsidiary Creditors. To protect all Creditors, the subsidiary filed bankruptcy in Delaware. To say the least, LaSalle's proposal was a severe conflict of interest. It appears that the subsidiary of a foreign bank does not believe that it is required to observe the ethics expected in the United States banking industry. It was recently announced that ABN AMRO will be fortunate if they are repaid 30% of their defaulted Argentina loans.

Shortly thereafter, A's Illinois subsidiary filed a $300 million suit against LaSalle Business Credit. The bankruptcy was filed in Delaware to avoid Judge Schneider, who had displayed complete bias in the earlier decision regarding the Winterland subsidiary.

While the Illinois subsidiary was in bankruptcy, A experienced more conflicts in the Judicial System than it ever realized existed. Its Illinois subsidiary's bankruptcy trustee had a three-year relationship with the New Jersey firm of Riker, Danzig, supposedly representing the unsecured Creditors of the Illinois subsidiary. Riker, Danzig at one time had also represented LaSalle Bank, and appeared more concerned about the bank's desires, and a continuing relationship, than for the unsecured Creditors that they were representing.

The bank was able to complete its original plan. It eliminated the Illinois subsidiary's Creditors, and had the assets sold to a company that the bank financed. Piper, Rudnick (formerly Piper Marbury), the firm that gave advice to company A during the Winterland acquisition in California, became the local counsel to Riker, Danzig, creating two conflicts. The purchaser of the Illinois subsidiary, in conjunction with the bank, was completely unsuccessful in operating the company, and the bank not only lost the opportunity to be paid off completely by the acquisition and financing that X's son had arranged, but lost a substantial amount of its original loan as well.

The Delaware Bankruptcy was unfortunately moved to Judge Schneider's court, who is the judge who dismissed the substantial suit against the two lenders to Winterland that caused the domino effect severely harming 2,484 parties.

The judge rescheduled hearings with no notice to A's shareholders or witnesses, and did nothing when the bank's attorneys participated in the withholding and destruction of documents needed by A to present its defense and handle the suit against the bank. The Assistant Acting U.S. Trustee cooperated with the Trustee's local counsel (Daneker, McIntire, Schumm, Prince, Goldstein, Manning & Widmann), in withholding and destroying the documents. While the local counsel had the only key to A's offices, substantial documents and personal art objects disappeared and the local police, the State's Attorney and Attorney General refused to investigate.

Miles & Stockbridge became local counsel for the Illinois bank, creating their third conflict.

Judge Schneider placed A in an unnecessary and questionable Chapter 7. A had only filed bankruptcy because it was a Delaware corporation, and wanted to get Delaware jurisdiction for its Illinois subsidiary, and to avoid similar biases demonstrated by Judge Schneider in an earlier dismissal of another suit.

At a hearing on August 22, 2002, A's counsel represented to the court that the Oklahoma City law firm of Federman & Sherwood would continue the $300 million suit against the bank on a completely contingent basis. A had no other creditors other than X's family. Judge Schneider denied the offer of a completely contingent continuation of the suit against the bank, and allowed the $300 million case, that would have repaid all creditors, to be sold to the bank at the shocking disparity of $2,500.

Judge Schneider approved Zvi Guttman as A's trustee, in the unnecessary Chapter 7 bankruptcy. The trustee had agreed with the counsel of a shareholder of A, to have an auction of the company's lawsuit against the bank, which the trustee originally agreed to and then reversed. He called the shareholders' attorney the next day and apologized, saying that this is what Judge Schneider wanted him to do and he had to do what the judge desired, because this is the way he earned his living. The shareholders' attorney relayed this conversation and is willing to testify to it. Notwithstanding the laws specifying the behavior of trustees, two trustees were so beholden to Judge Schneider, that they could not follow the Act approved by Congress.

In 2003, A and LaSalle settled on a walk away settlement. Almost concurrently with this settlement, Judge Schneider on June 13, 2003, belatedly issued a Memorandum of Judgment against X on the suit filed on August 13, 1999, by Venable on behalf of the Indenture Trustee. Judge Schneider's Memorandum stated that no attorneys or witnesses of A were believable, and everything alleged by Venable was accepted as fact. This is as incredible a situation, as when Venable was representing a large troubled savings and loan association, and at the same time was representing the Maryland state agency that guaranteed deposits in savings and loan associations, a severe conflict.

Appeals presented were denied by Federal District Court Judges who were former partners of Venable. The Judge's summary was not only fictional, but maintained that, remarkably, the five capable and experienced law firms employed by A during X's illness, issued incorrect advice and all documentation was misleading and incorrect. The judge blamed all of this on X, who was ill and not available at the time. The judge's June 13, 2003 Memorandum severely criticized the handling and opinions rendered by Piper, Rudnick of the 1996 Winterland acquisition, but Piper refused to object. This did not prevent Piper from being local counsel to Riker, Danzig, another obvious conflict. X has been attempting to continue these actions pro se, but per the beginning of this exposé, the court system is ignoring his motions.

X did not receive Judge Schneider's Memorandum of Judgment, which was incorrectly addressed, until July 3, 2003, during a pancreatic-related illness, and the local Judicial System refused to allow any leeway to file a late appeal.

The Foundation took certain actions of its own in the Fourth Circuit Court of Appeals to no avail. It requested that Judge Schneider be removed from the bench, and on December 1, 2003 the Richmond Appeals Court denied the motion, and the Foundation was not informed until February of 2004, that if it objected to the decision, such objection had to be filed by December 31, 2003. The Foundation wrote a letter to the judge handling the matter, which letter was never answered.

The Judicial System found its target in X. They indicted him, incarcerated him, embarrassed him, wounded him severely, took his hard-earned funds, caused 2,483 creditors to lose substantial funds, prevented a $75 million donation for cancer research, but to the benefit of 2,483 other Creditors, did not kill him.

The damage done by the Judicial System with all of its conflicts and biases, destroyed a business enterprise, hurt innocent bystanders, prevented a federally insured bank from being completely repaid, and created substantial legal fees.

The actions, notwithstanding, did not correct the damage done to A's subsidiaries, which A's organization would have corrected themselves, had they been allowed to.

7

Don't Wound the King, Kill Him!

The Foundation has stepped forward as a "stout-hearted man." It will diligently continue its efforts to collect the $75 million usurped from it by the Judicial System. It will make efforts to raise additional funds to research and cure cancer, as well as funds to cure the more manageable cancer in the Judicial System.

It is attracting additional volunteers to help in its efforts. Pending his health, X will help the Foundation in every way that he can. Two public relations firms, in different areas of expertise, have volunteered to help tell the Foundation's story.

A law firm has been located that will bring the necessary actions on behalf of the 2,484 Creditors. Twenty-five of the Creditors have volunteered to be named as specific plaintiffs as well.

The preceding exposé describes what has happened to 2,484 entities. Such sporadic abortions of the Judicial System happen every day. No one has been willing to stand up and demand changes, which the Foundation is doing.

The corrections that must be made vacillate between civil and criminal litigation. The trial of Martha Stewart can be referred to as part of the "Criminalization of America." Laws are passed that unknowingly will be violated. The Rules and Regulations under which United States citizens must live are being increased. Jails are being filled, and new ones are being built to house a new brand of legislated criminals.

If you are a minority, you are a candidate to be criminalized. If you are financially unable to defend a false charge, you are a candidate. If you have ever been in the public eye, you are a candidate. If you have had a successful career and your leadership in the community has been recognized, you are a candidate. Anyone could become an inmate in the growing "American Gulag." You could even unknowingly be placed on the "dirty trick" list of the FBI.

If you fit any of these categories, you could be indicted, convicted and jailed for crimes you did not commit. You will be guilty until proven innocent, if proven innocent. You could be ridiculed by the press. Your life and business could be destroyed. You could pour out your financial lifeblood to defend yourself and still lose. And then you will become a convicted felon with all of the related indignities, although it is possible this is changing with the recent attitude of the public toward Martha Stewart.

In 1990, fifty-four well-known congressmen sponsored a bill know as H.R. 4079. Included in that group were congressmen Ginghrich, Condit, Lukins, and Molinari, to name a few. The bill would have turned the Republican Party's holy war against drugs into a national emergency. This bill would have required drug users to perform work at less than minimum wages, which would parallel the "slave labor" employed at the Krupps Steelworks in Germany during World War II. It would have permitted housing tents on military bases, which are no different from the concentration camps that Americans criticize so severely. Fortunately this bill did not pass.

The U.S. Judicial System is truly an awesome force in our society. When the powers of prosecutors and judges are misdirected, which occasionally they are, it can result in a complete destruction of an innocent person's life. Justice Department officials have wide leeway to grant immunity, negotiate plea bargains, develop perjured evidence, and are encouraged to violate the Canons of Legal Ethics. When Governor Thornburg was Attorney General, in a written policy, he encouraged prosecutors to negotiate plea bargains behind the backs of defense lawyers. He instructed his prosecutors to do anything necessary to get convictions. It was no longer important who was innocent or guilty, correct or incorrect, but who wins.

The Office of Professional Responsibility has been mentioned. It over and over again whitewashes anything that is done by employees of the Justice Department. It receives fifty to sixty allegations of prosecutorial abuse each year, and does not aggressively pursue them. It has never recommended the firing of a Federal prosecutor for abusing his or her position, even when the misconduct has been cited by a Federal judge. It is a joke to say that the Justice Department polices itself. It doesn't! It shields itself.

Many Federal judges are appointed for life and help prosecutors. Too many indictments result in convictions while not only prosecutorial but judicial misconduct runs rampant. Federal judges can be impeached for high crimes and misdemeanors, but not for unacceptable and biased behavior, incompetence or mental illness. The system is deteriorating under the gavels of judges who join and support the prosecutors. As early as 1941, the House passed a bill providing for a judicial proceeding that could remove a Federal judge. The Foundation has been unable to document one removal. In 1978, the Senate voted to establish a court on Judicial Conduct and Disability with powers to remove and censor judges. Both bills died in the other chamber. To add insult to injury, after someone is improperly indicted and convicted, the appeal process is usually a farce.

Martha Stewart was correct in going to jail first and getting on with her life, obviously recognizing that fact. Many innocent victims sit in jail while a slow Judicial System finds ways to deny and not consider the appeals. Judges do not like to be judged. They glory in their independence. The system must demand that there be no bad judges left on the bench, if we are to have a true justice system under our democracy.

The Supreme Court, several years ago, ruled that judges do not have authority to police prosecutorial misconduct. This leaves convictions in the hands of overzealous prosecutors, who are anxious to get another notch on their guns.

The enigma of the American Judicial System is the crime of perjury. In most countries it is not a crime. During almost every legal case, someone commits perjury. A judge or jury then determines which story is most creditable. Seldom does a perjury charge result from a court case. Every member of the human race tells a lie or distorts the truth sometime during every day of their lives. When a prosecutor arranges for or coerces government witnesses to perjure themselves it is still perjury. The fear of being charged with perjury prevents most people from appearing before Grand Juries which are controlled by prosecutors and not by the confused little old men and women in their tee shirts and tennis shoes who are selected to serve. Prosecutors tell Grand Jurors how to vote and they do as told most of the time.

Civil litigation has more problems than criminal, because of the large number of civil cases, versus criminal cases.

The 75th Congress established a very comprehensive set of Federal Rules of Civil Procedure, 86 in all. Many judges and lawyers in the Judicial System do not abide by those rules. One infraction in one area can multiply to a cancer that can destroy the entire system. The Supreme Court has shown no concern for the violation of those 86 Rules. Violation of those Rules cost the Foundation and 2,483 other people, over $335 million.

The violations of those Rules furthermore have delayed the most important thing that the Foundation can do, and that is to prevent those five hundred thousand people who are going to die each year from meeting that fate. Also, the Foundation wants to reduce the number of people in the United States who suffer from cancer.

Do not turn your back on Judicial cancer. It can affect 300,000,000 people, not just 100,000,000, like physical cancer. It does not end your life, but makes it not worth living.

Dissimilar to other authors, other exposés, and elected officials who do not answer correspondence or return telephone calls, the Foundation will be available to answer questions and correspondence. The back cover of this book shows where to address correspondence, that will be promptly answered, as well as where to place telephone calls for immediate conversations.

The "stout-hearted" Foundation and the Creditors ask for your support.

THE END

0-595-34745-2

www.ingramcontent.com/pod-product-compliance
Lightning Source LLC
Chambersburg PA
CBHW021244280526

45784CB00005B/2230